NEW CANADIAN POETS SERIES

This series of titles from Quarry Press charts new directions being taken in contemporary Canadian poetry by presenting the first book-length work of innovative writers.

Other titles in the series include *Undressing the Dark* by Barbara Carey, *The Big Life Painting* by Ron Charach, *Stalin's Carnival* by Steven Heighton, *The Speed of the Wheel Is Up to the Potter* by Sandy Shreve, and *The Untidy Bride* by Sandra Nicholls.

The River & The Lake

Poetry & Drawings by

Joanne Page

Quarry Press

Copyright © Joanne Page, 1993.

All rights reserved.

The publisher gratefully acknowledges the assistance of The Canada Council, the Ontario Arts Council, the Department of Communications, and the Ontario Publishing Centre.

Canadian Cataloguing in Publication Data

Page, Joanne
The river & the lake: poetry and drawings

(New Canadian poets series)
ISBN 1-55082-090-7

I. Title.   II. Series.

PS8581.A383R49 1993   C811'.54   C93-090494-X
PR9199.3.P34R49 1993

Cover art by the author.
Design by Keith Abraham.
Typesetting by Quarry Press, Inc.

Printed and bound in Canada by Webcom, Toronto, Ontario.

Published by
Quarry Press, Inc.,
P.O. Box 1061, Kingston, Ontario.

the place we end up in
goes deeper than choice, if we're lucky.

Bronwen Wallace, "Seeing is Believing"

For Ian, Geoff and Steve

THE RIVER

What the eye sees is a dream of sight
what it wakes to
is a dream of sight

    W.S. Merwin, "To the Hand"

Black Ice

To the west the hill rises sharply,
shoulders hunched, allowing the river to freeze
smooth if a cold snap comes
before snow, and if it lasts
you can skate from Hull's Dam
under the bridge at Dundas Street
all the way to Stanley Park on ice
black as arctic night
crystal-cut with white slashes
angling down this way
and that, among sleeping fish
through descending lines of infinitely smaller bubbles —
gems on a jeweller's cloth,
fronds held in the dark
until thaw.

Lie right down on the ice,
face close to the sticky cold surface,
your breath curling steamy over the river
now halted altogether and heavy
with the effort of standing still
when every river is pulled,
pushing to go on.
Wait for the beat of your heart to slow,
enough to hear the light tatter-music
weeds make without wind
and finally
a great boom
as the river draws breath.

Of Mills

Forget at your peril
that this is a place
determined by its past.
Tamed and sluggish, the West Credit
still powers the wheel
of the mill Daniel MacMillan built
in 1838, to grind oats
into good Scots stick-to-the-ribs
porridge, fuel for those first
boat people who claimed the land
and died young.
A little downstream
was Cornock's, also in grain,
his distillery causing and easing sorrow
as the forest came down
for ridge poles in barns,
then planking in granaries
all the way to Hillsburg
after Ben Mundell bought the mill
in '96, and went into lumber.

They were some builders then,
Daniel raised five mills
two raceways and a house,
(mostly stone from Shingler's quarry)
before he died at thirty-eight.
The wheel turned
and turned, while Ben
kept careful records — *four
fan lights over bedroom doors
at three dollars each, for Overland's,*
Ben marking his time
in the ledger, in brick
and stone on Main Street.

By the time we built,
Mundell's was Home Hardware,
packed with coffee makers,
barbecues, patio furniture,
as well as wood.
Young Bill Corbett ran rough-cut
hemlock through Ben's planer;
the days he farmed
Slim took over, Slim lean enough
to make me wonder if he'd slipped through
himself one idle afternoon.
A wet summer,
the roof raised in falling snow,
and we would never have made it
except Bill and Jim carried us
for a while,
perhaps mindful of Ben's last entry:
Death evens all Debts.

**The River
&
The Lake**

Putting In Time

for Fred McLaren

Annie Mae has died and gone to heaven
where she is making raisin pies
for Fred; in time he'll be along
needing a meal, cup of something hot
after the trip. I don't suppose
she will be lonely — heaven
must be full of Presbyterians —
but she surely will miss Fred
and the old brick house
by the fair grounds.
You get used to a place,
the way the light falls
through the front window
of a winter morning, weak
and soft — as though it could not creep
across the floor to the other wall,
as though it barely made it this far —
used to the feel of stair planks
centre-worn and giving underfoot,
the scent of toast, a suggestion
of calla lilies around the walls.
It's probably very nice
in heaven, all shiny and gold,
but I know she'll keep an eye open
for that nose of Fred's, for his hat,
carefully watch when she's here and there
pursuing her celestial business,
looking for the special way
he walks, leaning back,
his feet drawing him forward
as though they had holiday travel
plans that the rest of him
didn't know about.
He'll show up grinning
when she least expects him,
hands in his pockets
just back from down-street
with the mail.

The Meeting

for Ruth Meek

Chores done, the men have gone to town
ahead of the storm
leaving barn clothes
and straw-covered boots sentinel
to add the fragrance of today's new piglets
to the smell of Rice Crispie squares,
Nanaimo bars,
butterscotch cookies and coffee
brewing in the kitchen.

The women of The Institute gather
in Ruth's front room,
open the meeting with the song their mothers sang,
arrange themselves in a circle
as women will
when children are asleep
or away,
and while they will discuss
saving pennies for wells
in Bangladesh, or an afternoon
of euchre in Brampton, and maybe write
a letter to the Premier protesting Sunday shopping,
what sticks
is how Aggie cried
and couldn't read the card
they'd signed in the kitchen,
beautiful roses
In Sympathy, for Chuck,
only son, just twenty-five,
killed on an oil rig last month,
and the way Ruth woke Mrs. Finlayson
gently — she always nodded off during the speaker —
so she wouldn't miss tea,
everyone gathering to get away
before they found themselves storm-stayed.

**The River
&
The Lake**

Progress

Every village main street worth its salt
boasts one brick hotel
remaindered from the days
when moving twenty miles across country
was a day's work, then fitted up with
every kind of business
save undertaking and worship,
those having been accounted for
from the beginning.

In my day
The Bush went from hostelry
to pub, Harleys out front
and raunchy movies flickering over the bar.
That incarnation eventually yielded
to fine country dining, and Black George
wouldn't know it if he came back
from wherever it was he went when he died.

Black George wasn't black, merely dirty
and drunk most of the time
when he lived on the top floor.
No one in town was black except one man
rumoured to be a drug dealer
from New York, who sat in a big car
outside the high school,
eventually making off with
our neighbour's second daughter.

That was how little we understood
of the world then — black men
came from the States, that she could not
have gone willingly, that hotels
were places for guests to stay.

Transgression

Striking out over the speckled land,
the boys go hunting down the eighth line
just as they always have,
except that Bert has had a hip replaced
and Al has cataracts;
the field is surrounded
by estate housing lots now,
each running around half a million.

One reminds the other
of the time the young hounds
got away on them,
tore the neighbour's kitten to shreds
and backed the woman down the road up
against her log house in the rain,
after her coon coat.

Old Wilson is stationed
at the truck
with the beer,
in case the deer breaks
they tell him,
but really it's because he's too old
to get back in the hills anymore
but won't stay home.
A neighbour passes
in his brand-new fourwheel drive,
deep in cellular conversation
about trespass laws, ignoring
Old Wilson as he waves,
gun on forearm,
one foot on the bumper,
one foot in the field.

White on White

Maybe the best time
is the last week in March
when water moves
under sugar snow
so you can hear it emptying
into ditches,
swelling the marsh
on both sides
as you walk toward the twisty hill
half the town wants to straighten.

If you know where to look
there is a creek
in the maple bush glistening
with watercress,
slicing its way
under a lick of ice etched
from the edge as though
set by a glazier,
moving winter downstream
over the escarpment
through cataracts
to the lake,
clearing way
for a sweep of trillium
so white
you would swear
the hemisphere had tumbled,
and winter newly arrived.

The River
&
The Lake

In April

for Mary Footman

Rosy light touches snow
in a spring pond:
runoff, really,
thaw puddle hollowed
into the hill,
with indigo shadows
and drowned thorn bushes,
two ducks floating
above their replicas.
Preoccupied, I have no time
for this as I drive away
from a dying friend
who loves this hilly road we share
and must leave it.
The ducks rise silently
straight up,
clarified by flight
I am lifted to a kind of minor joy:
here, this momentary grace
will survive us.

Confidence

Only little things at first,
hepatica placed carefully
in leaf cover, shoots of wild leek
underfoot; the hardwood bush
is frugal in spring,
as a country woman will take care
how much she says
until she knows you better, the offerings
small — like how she hates
her son and his pal driving the truck
around Saturday nights
up and down the town line
with an open case of beer —
waiting to hear what you say
watching to see if you shake your head
slightly, enough to tell her
you know how much she worries,
how scared she is his dad will
find out, not enough to damn
the lad as a reckless fool
because God knows
all the boys do it.

After a season
she might get more generous:
she'll let go,
talk about the guy she almost married
who farms the other side of Cedar Valley
and how maybe if things weren't so bad
at home, the bank loan, John
so unpredictable, raging at the boys all the time,
she wouldn't have gone to meet him
in the bush behind his barn
last week, just to talk.

The River
&
The Lake

        She'll cry telling
        how the woods were full
        of gilded ruby columbine and blue flags
        blowing in dry pond-grass
        and the fire of Indian paintbrush
        blazing right out of the trees
        into the field.
        She'll close her eyes
        firmly, as chicory
        closes its blue fringed rays
        at midday,
        shutting out the long shadows.

Stabat Mater

Florence at the fashion show
in the church basement
where she customarily
served egg salad sandwiches
after funerals or watched babies
in the nursery when no one else would,
but this time decked out,
walking between tables of women,
turning, turning
as if she had done it all her life.

Something inordinately lovely
shone in her face,
pleasure maybe
in the sweep of rosy sleeves against her arms,
but probably more to do with seven kids
and years of cooking lunch
for the high school cafeteria
after Frank's stroke,
hanging on,
never complaining —
you just didn't —
worrying about groceries
and winter boots,
then watching one
by one leave
for Barrie, Fergus, B. C.
and Orangeville to raise kids, hold down
decent jobs, some going as far as
Ecuador to do God's work among the Indians.

No one left at home
but Frank and Frank's cousin
with them years on end.
Time enough for moments
when nothing on earth matters more
than the sound of silk.

Matters of Belief

Back then there were six churches,
four on the main street,
The Living Word
out on the highway,
and the Catholics
around the corner on Mill Street,
their parish hall
a portable, as though
the lesser parts of the faith
could be relocated at a moment's notice.

We were Presbyterian, occupying the biggest
and therefore the most empty of these churches
raised in more certain times
before God died
or became uneasy with His gender.
We talked more of heating bills
than redemption, the faithful pitting
souls against septic beds,
which led to a certain confusion in my mind
on the maintenance of salvation
and large buildings.

The unexpected gift of money
to sandblast the bricks and fix the roof —
was that evidence of the mystery?
or Sunday morning light, cobalt and scarlet,
on worn faces offered
to the colours as to blessing —
was that it? — or was it
not in there at all,
but out back, a hot night's haze of fireflies
over Queen Anne's lace,
extravagant solstice lighting
on loan
from the firmament.

Haying

for Mary and John Thacker

Four days of pure July heat
and we would pile in the truck
and help with the haying at the barn
over near Caledon
(built round in '98
so no farmer could be cornered
by the devil).
The kids chased the tractor
or rode on the truck cab
in t-shirts, shorts and winter mitts,
limbs rashed from jumping
in the domed loft
and raising dust motes under rafters
rayed out in perfect intervals
like hymn notes.

Borrowed baler,
weather shifts,
the calculating was always rush against risk.
We hauled bales off
the wagon, on to the rickety
elevator, off the top,
through speckled light shafts,
salted and set them in levels,
cubes in a circle, geometry as uneasy
as the question: was the stacked-
fast hay cured,
and the barn safe?

Half a year later,
it burned to its circular source
in December rain —
the devil, of course,
has all the time in the world.

**The River
&
The Lake**

Dancers

Fred and Myrtle are dancing
sweeping over the Legion floor
slick as wax, waltzing
with assurance, cutting a swath
around the edge of the crowd
where the real dancers always go
and everyone makes room, stepping
back, clapping, while Fred
and Myrtle go round as they used to
before Myrtle's feet got so bad
that she couldn't help
with church luncheons anymore,
although the laundry still goes out
the line billowing
over yellow Steen's trucks
pairs and pairs of jeans drying
in the updraft
from the bakery next door, bread-
filled, donut, danish and wholewheat air
rising over town at eleven,
every morning but Monday.

Myrtle and Fred dance
in smokey light
skaters on a wooden pond
they might be young again,
time rendered insubstantial
by their ceaseless motion
and Jeff Barry's music rising
like yeast,
warm, rich, undeniable.

Stanley Park

Pat O'Sullivan could never hear the noise,
Evelyn could.
Night after night
the new fibreglass plant
across the CPR tracks
kept her awake,
until she could only sleep
with earplugs
and the windows shut,
not catching the slap of beaver tail
or spring peepers in the weeds
at the foot of the lawn
where it ran up against the pond,
never hearing radios,
dogs barking and kids crying
in trailers across the water in
Stanley Park.

They say it was a fine sight
of a summer eighty years ago.
Two storey cottages circled the edge,
each with balcony and boathouse,
afternoons thick with polished boats
pointed front and back;
men in straw hats
girls in fine lawn gowns
carried on pavilion music,
rowing slowly, as dust
from the racetrack
drifts through slanting sun.
The park was famous then.
Families came from town by train
drawn up the Credit valley
across the bridge at the long turn
by Belfountain and Brimstone
on to Cataract,
the river strong enough
to generate power
and flood in spring.

They came for dances and gatherings,
for hot summer evenings
when the last of the ice lay under sawdust
small as the memory
of January in August, reduced,
as outings at the park
eventually were.

Evelyn sold up and moved to Guelph
after Pat died,
some said taking a loss,
some said just to get away,
leaving behind one wooden cross
among all the granite and limestone
to mark the passing of a son
who died before heart surgery
got as routine as train travel
and horse races used to be.

Over time, rules were changed
and the plant boss
made to get the noise in hand,
leaving the park
insulated, quiet again,
a reverie of cottages and mobile homes
going nowhere.

**The River
&
The Lake**

Changing of the Guard

Milly and Lloyd surrendered
the family grocery business
suddenly, around the time,
must have been soon after
Milly fell in the chest freezer
and busted her arm but
Lloyd, it was said, never took much
to provisioning anyway
so it was no great loss.
Buckets of Bing cherries and syrup,
cornstarch and pectin
disappeared overnight as did Lloyd
for a while, freed to fish
and pursue more northern prey,
his store stocked with books
on steam trains
and derelict railways.

On the other hand
Bill Bush you'll see
sitting by the window
of what used to be his store
in a captain's chair
the new owner thoughtfully
supplied, waving at shapes his eyes
shroud in fog,
saving him the bother of spotting
friend among strangers —
everything in town fairly strange
these days to old Bill —
his nail-and-screw life
replaced by disposable diapers
and lottery tickets,
ephemeral solutions and poor odds.

River

for Tracy Howlett

The far side of the dam
a swinging tree remains
where one June
a decade ago, kids,
boys mostly, fixed rope
to perfectly located limb
and spent every afternoon
seeing who could jump out the furthest.
Tracy watched from shore
babysitting, (paying off
a blue-quilted, catalogue coat)
till it got so hot she looked out
an old inner tube,
floated out with the twins to watch,
got into the splashing,
they slipped off, all three,
twins hung on but she was lost
until they found her
plastered up against the grating
under the dam.

A sweep of maple keys
rattled, restless on the church steps
as a friend stood on a pew
and lined the family up
around the casket,
taking pictures
so we wouldn't forget.
We sang *Amazing Grace How Sweet It Is*
as loud as we could, to drown
the day's insupportable flaw: her hair,
done all wrong, back from her forehead
instead of bangs.

The River
&
The Lake

Waterlilies,
white fingers reaching
straining through umber
and green — the strongest colour —
to keep from being pulled under.

This is the end of the summer now
and the river scarcely moves;
thick with mud
it leans heavily against banks
high enough to bear the weight of dark water
and its final lilies spread out
floating.

Annie

Miss Annie Cook of Centre Street
stands beside her seven foot high trumpet lily
in yellowed newsprint.
My notebook records the event
eight years after frost.
She smiles at me, tiny by the lilies
and I wish I could hear her voice,
not remotely floral,
pitched low, as though compressed.

I saw her first years ago in a storm,
wind blowing Armageddon
and she bent, leaned into the blast,
gathered sticks from my lawn
dense with kindling,
stopping long enough to tell me
that my house had been hers when she was a child,
and I thought of her that summer
when my redheaded son playing in the garden
found a 1904 copper.

Miss Annie Cook of Centre Street grows her bulbs in summer
shops every day at four,
tends her ancestors' stones
tilted cemetery wildness,
pioneers, founders, kinsmen, mill-builders, quarrymen,
saddlers, and mothers of five who lived and four who died,
all now in her safekeeping
until the blossoms turn to brass.

The Fair

Elwood doesn't go at all anymore
whereas I wouldn't miss it,
which probably reflects the number of times
each of us
has watched the Clydes
or listened to Sam Leitch fiddle
over the years, or looked in those
wood and glass cases at mustard pickles,
the kind with pearl onions,
best pies, all short the slice
taken in Friday judging.
It's Erin Fair time again.
My kids will lose
most of their summer wood-stacking money
on the crown and anchor game,
eat United Church hot dogs
bring home three goldfish in pink water
who will die inside a week.

On Saturday morning
Flossie sits at the seniors' table,
regal under the prizewinners, selling
tickets on a quilt
while not hearing much
which does not bother her especially
as outside ten tractors roar, pulling
their weight and more
on a track furrowed
after rain.
Maybe the rides
are a little more rickety this year,
but hey, we aren't running Wonderland here,
just the best fair in the province.

I think I began to understand
the way oldtimers felt about us
when I was elbowed aside
by a man in country clothes too clean
to ever have seen the inside of a barn,
and heard his kids complain about the smell
of Blythe Meek's pigs, the ones that would clean
up next month
at the Royal.
They were gone by four
without another thought
of candyfloss and spotless pigs
never to know how hard Blythe, Ruth
and the five kids worked
to make them that way.
Of course you don't discover
things like that in an afternoon,
or even a couple of months.

Belonging is a covenant
between place and person
requiring time,
years of staying on,
being there until someone
lets you help with the dishes
or pile up sandbags when the river
overflows the dam at Charles Street,
featureless, easeful as sanity,
belonging is the jig
Sam bows for you
in a near-empty beer tent.

The River
&
The Lake

Over Coffee

There's what you talk about
but really
it's what you know that forms the rock
you build conversations on,
solid as elbows on the table
over coffee.

The story isn't that Anderson
is getting careless, planting his grain
a couple of inches too deep,
so much as the chemo he's been having
in Hamilton most of the winter
is pretty much a waste of time.
It's in the family,
his sister Allie has it too — breast —
and looks poorly again, the grey
that should have nothing whatever to do with skin
and makes you look away
quickly, grabbing seconds
to let your features rearrange themselves
into a flat unknowing surface,
a slab of granite
before the chisel.

It's Dorry, his wife, running around
on him, turning up at the Legion Thursday night
after mixed baseball with that kid
who works the line for Hydro.
Somebody at Cedar Valley
saw her car driving into Bob's laneway
a couple of times last summer,
so it probably isn't the first time;
well, sure it's hard on her —
John's got a fine temper
hasn't he, and these last few months
he's been sending good money after bad
buying that tractor he doesn't need —
but she's not dying, is she?

And what about the oldest boy
bashing mailboxes with the truck
on weekends, pissed to the gills,
and everyone asking about it
Monday morning on the Post Office steps, as if
they didn't know it's Charlie?
Of course maybe it isn't,
so why not give him the benefit —
why not keep quiet,
give the kid a break?
He'll settle down
in a couple of years, hell
he's already lost his job
and who knows how much longer his dad will last?
It's not so much protection
as keeping a lid on
what people actually say out loud.

Words have a way of gathering,
falling like a blight on a field
of oats, leaving nothing
but dry husks
and bleached stones in the furrows.

***The River
&
The Lake***

Shut out in the Garden

for Jean Marshall

If you didn't know them
you would drive by smiling
sure they must be happy,
Jean and Bill in their garden
finest in town
right at the corner of the highway
where you can't miss it,
grey heads bent over empty rows
taking up the last of the carrots
digging out tangled
root systems, cutting back
overgrown currants
as the end of the season
blows around them
wild with leaves.

Kids gone, she quit teaching
nine years ago.
She needed to learn
to paint, big canvases
of meadowrue, ladyslipper, bluebells,
and she wanted to travel,
but Bill wouldn't go,
because of the weeding, he said,
but she knew better,
understood he was scared to go away
from what he did best;
he'd been that way
since that first year
when his back was broken
and they lost the farm.

So he stayed put
when she drove to the city,
selling old cars, chairs,
barrels, junk in the driveway
to passing cottagers,
watching Friday traffic from his porch,
drinking rye, phoning old friends
in the evening, asking, "where's Jean?"
until, finally, she gave up
classes, plans, stayed home
with sunflowers and winter birds,
dreaming of blood red poppies in Provence
and Amazon butterflies
that drink turtles' tears.

Auction

It was fall and
Morris wore
his blue jacket, brown hat,
stood in the yard
of his house
beside the hotel,
watched city people
pick up and put down his garden rake,
listened to his daughter-in-law
and neighbour bid up the price
of the dining room table
brought here when the farm sold ten years before
for a price that took his breath away.
Chests, chairs,
piles of quilts,
beds arranged at intervals
on the grass, each singular,
apparently unrelated to the next
as mourners at the graveside will stand
spread out, still
with loss.
When it was over
he followed dealers and friends
as they lugged their loot
to the street
interred the pieces of his life
in trunks and trucks
drove away,
left him standing
on the square of lawn
that buried his garden
the kind that only retired farmers grow
when they move to town,
weedless, matchless turnips,
feathery carrots in rows
purple onions, jungle of squash leaves,
hills of potatoes
swelling under his feet,
green tomatoes
in the dark, ripening.

The River
&
The Lake

The Hill

Beech trees hang on to
bronze leaves
long after October
has cleaned the maples bare.
There are one or two big ones
just over the ridge, back from the dump
which smolders
sending out undecipherable signals —
perhaps distress —
once or twice a week.
Two paths lead over the top,
one through a confusion
of wild grape and bindweed
to a lane, then across
pastures where Mr. Little's Herefords
consort occasionally
with a Highlander,
careless of the shaggy results
grazing nearby;
the other leads south
along the top
then dips down
sharply enough to make you tack
back and forth across the bare face
to keep your footing,
leveling out at a deer meadow
trembling with goldenrod spears
and royal purple aster stars:
the last offering
before wind drives
hue entirely away.

Guardians

Dolly and Flora
layed back the skin
of this place
like surgeons,
when town was where you came
after Friday supper for nails,
a yard of stout cloth
after weeklong chores and ploughing,
to catch the news Dolly and Flora
circulated through their switchboard,
pulsing system wired
to predilection and heartbeats.

Dolly, solitary in the house
at the cenotaph that every town
of two thousand has, commemorating old wars,
strewn with poppy wreaths
faded as the memories of those who knew
"our boys who died in France"
(in this instance, twenty-four).
Flora's Bert, first at the creamery,
then on to higher station —
town clerk of tax bills
and water payments,
privy to council minutes, but never knowing
as Flora and Dolly always did
as a matter of course,
where the doctor was
or who was cousin to anyone.

Dolly died, Bert's gone too.
Flora's bad hip keeps her home,
but when a new family begins to paint
the house across the street
layering a fresh approach
over dimmed and flaking yesterday,
she gives them nicely stitched
old tales of the days
when she and Dolly ran the phones,
keeping back the weathered secrets
carrying them on.

Ceremony

On the first weekend in December
when the temperature sits on zero
and rain decides whether or not to be snow,
most of the town lines the street
between the liquor store
and the old fire hall
to watch the parade.

The Georgetown pipe band, knees raw-red
as the music, follows Roy and Anne in the model T,
polished up like the harnesses on Braiden's Belgians,
Joe in the steam engine,
everyone waiting for him to pull the whistle
so they can cover their ears and scream.

The great thing is
it's the same every year:
Doug driving tractor,
hauling a load of Brownies
(though his mother died last night,
just dropped, like her sister before her),
the highway jammed with flatbeds,
transports, two firetrucks,
village council decked out
as Santa's elves, Santa's stagecoach
plugging weekend traffic up for a mile.

The River
&
The Lake

If you knew where to look
you might lift your eyes
and see the hill
but you wouldn't see the river
for the row of stores
that fasten their gaze on the street
and conceal the deepest secret
behind them, river, water-
way withheld and motionless,
hoary ice crystals, caught leaves
on flinty surface,
and beneath, clouds of lily-
tangle, dense as memory.

Even looking, you couldn't know
that Anne is wearing Tracy's
catalogue coat in the unheated Ford,
quilted blue arms embracing
what she can never forget,
or that Dorry left John alone on the farm.
Some choices lie at your feet, familiar
as the road home.
Others, like a river
bear you away without bargain
through glossy breadth of reach
and lake to sea,
its intertidal purpose.

THE LAKE

I was thinking:
so this is how you swim inward
so this is how you flow outward
so this is how you pray.

    Mary Oliver,
    "Five A.M. in the Pinewoods"

temagami, september

1. Reading

Canoes pulled up on shore,
the great lake calm
and hikers down from the ridge,
the weekend's collection
of old-hands and newcomers,
intent on penetrating
a rocky resistance
you might call
beginning to know the land.
they gather,
content to form
a rough circle of fire-lit listeners
in an old log lodge.

embraced by Temagami's vast wooden arms,
I put on reading glasses
to blur the fifty or so faces
open the worn book
introduce the poem, carefully
explain it's offered in memory
of one of last year's group
who died too young,
cancer I say, going on to
add that its author, my friend
(who also died)
wrote it for her friend,
who died
leaving four small children.
both of cancer, yes, I say quickly,
all three of cancer, in fact,
relieved they've caught
the interweave and theme
of my homily on death by cell division
and released me from the awful accretion
of dead women.

2. Beach

Poem given,
the room rearranges itself
and I see your face
behind the questioners,
in your eyes
wild appeal: *come with me.*
outside your sobs rise unbidden
from somewhere in here, you say,
touching the region of your heart,
hearts being the order of business
on this irregular weekend.
your tears on cooled sand,
a trail of dark circles behind us
as we walk a shore line
between who we are
and what we might be
in low uncritical light,
you, seized by unexpected grief —
not even yours —
me, bone-dry
in the way of empty earthenware vessels
left long in heat.

I am not like this, you say,
you'll think I'm crazy,
a possibility that seems remote
and of no consequence.

The River
&
The Lake

        we walk on,
        you crying,
        me wondering about
        all the years of grown-up
        work we do,
        most of us intent on
        searching out the limits
        of knowing
        so there will be no surprises,
        drawing a circumference
        around matters
        elusive as the pure instant
        when night turns into dawn.
        making allowance for emotion,
        even error,
        but seldom for mystery,
        that shadowland we lived in
        as children, without a notion
        of why unforeseen rescue
        or blame
        were equally possible
        in a given moment.
        all the years we spend
        moving on to the next territory,
        which always turns out to be
        a re-working of the same ground,
        like this beach
        drawing itself
        to a tapered conclusion.

        both spent, we turn,
        no further ahead
        than sudden, savage hunger.

3. Square Dance

Dinner dishes cleared,
the dining hall holds on for dear life
its purchase on the grassy flats
never entirely secure,
rafters and plank floor
imprinted with years of dancing
rigid geometry
to contain this wheeling hurricane of arms
legs and fiddle-playing,
impossible now to distinguish
novice from native
dancers all in the reckless equality
of whirling squares.

I stand in the storm's centre
gripped by its polar opposite,
an afternoon so burdened with knowledge
of its end
it scarcely moved,
minutes not passing
but floating in place
on morphine insufficient
to touch the pain
that gathered what
my friend fiercely hoarded
and set it in huge eyes,
moved them restlessly
from mine to the clock,
measuring time left
against what she could bear.

The River
&
The Lake

        this was the struggle then:
        she, dying,
        and I, companion
        to this vicious carcinoma riddle
        as though there were only
        one answer, one question;
        as if knowing
        whether I was placed
        beside her,
        motionless in a pine rocking chair,
        by chance or choice
        would make clear
        how to carry this irreducible sadness.

4. Departure

Last morning pack-up.
we are only passing through this forgiving land,
its insinuation of water over stone
air-turned birch leaves
reversing, over and over,
silver backs against a sky
necessary as change.
the procession of legs and knapsacks
snakes slowly along the edge
of blazing autumn bush:
the trail back.

alone, I'm drawn beachward
for one last look at the lake
laid flat as a bolt of blue linen
flung out for the sheer pleasure
of its weave.
I move cautiously,
never knowing when foot meets rock
which will hold,
as uncertain tips of fingers
will travel over a face
newly loved,
not yet trusted.
all around me ancient sites
of ritual and recollection
lifelines on the land
traced in footfall and blade,
invisible, insistent,
the wonder of how I came
to find myself alive
on this long arc of precambrian sand
holds me.
I travel blind.
overhead
the last of the geese
with their other ways of knowing
lift their miraculous feathers to the stars.

diagnosis, december

lump
right breast
malignant

small weight
shrill note
rubbed from crystal lip
discover music
and watch the world collapse
at once.

on a small craft
upriver
wreathed in everlasting
to float among clouds
& measure days
in crewel stitchery.

surgery
radiation
all beginning, to what end?

The River
&
The Lake

tumult, where i travel

a hoarse voice seizes me
sings rough cutting songs of bone
& pain until I can no more bear
      the notes
crammed tight
between staves, their linear draw
all that remains of forever,
a summoning
I know to be
the core of the matter.

bound, I am held
within a red pulse
which is the life I never thought
      of saving
waiting for rescue.
ashes rise around me,
the brute flame rages
and heat burns my every ringing cell.

I long for a coolness
enough to lay myself down in,
like a child in the crook of her mother's arm
like fear into prayer.

knife

the line of my life a snapped
          string

rind of skin
new-stitched and pink
insignia
that the bead of death
is cut away
does not banish
the grey corruption of fear
    huddled like shaped spectres
        in the eyes of my sons.

I am split:
promise of taken on one side,
mystery of given
         on the other,

my dark and gleaming centre
laid open.

*The River
&
The Lake*

edge

for Pam Benson

I'll tell you how I see our relationship
developing, she says as the gardener
in her takes shears to my confusion,
the way it works is that it's my job to take care
of you and not yours to take care of me,
I won't drop around for tea
which isn't to say
that I wouldn't like to,
we won't be friends
you might need me again.

I shiver, wrapped in her shawl,
spread of creamy wool
edged with intricate borders, subtle tracery,
the job is, of course
to work my death
into my life.

only a waterline between us
shore indistinguishable
pierced
by reeds
vertical entries
into the still liquid
of motion contained.
a thistle seed cartwheels by
on surface tension,
its thousand downy limbs burst
in aortal light.

before spring

the road to the lake in one turn
will skirt the barn, the drive-shed,
part two cut fields,
    run down bare rock
     spining a bronze hill,
move flat along the spread of beaver work —
meadow and spongy humps
& gnawed sticks wind dried —
    hiding the fork.

    go right.

    a borrowed thing,
the lake road knows no purpose
       but to divine,
    no precision
beyond the accuracy of getting there,
    this company of packed dirt
a way to waiting, to the continuous

i stand and shade my eyes

to uncompromising blue ether breath
behind land laid out across water
as far up as I can lean back,
then black cedar horizon
and closer,
mauve, rose, even gold
rounding into scrubbed form,
here breasts, there belly,
deep red dogwood veins mark life
strangers bend and snap
without thought of blood.

a modest acreage
fixed to mind,
thorns narrowing to a point:
remember this

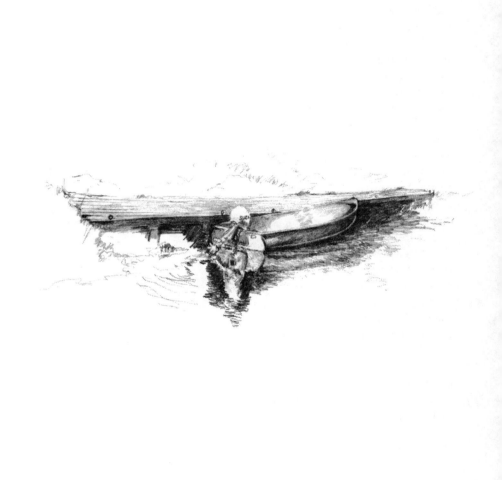

early

outboard engines
covered like cages
and the lake before breakfast
is glass a loon call might crack
only swallows
to give you faith in flying.

the heron in place
upright on the rock
eyes me, dares me
doubt the guise of weathered wood

and I,
as still in my canoe,
wonder at how she keeps herself
to grey-blue intent —
   burnished shoal
   search.

she lifts off suddenly, tearing
lavender air with
the ragged stab of her call,
(as if it were newly given
and this its debut).
heft and blur of her tipped feathers
   hold,
      shearing off
into bright upper register,
the simmering canopy that is morning
parts, takes her in.

The River
&
The Lake

inland

the birch alone
among a crowd of conifers
suggests with its stroke of white
an answer.

a staghorn sumach
crowns our hill,
angular birdfeeder
wearing a slow activity
of pine grosbeaks
around its rufous fruit
and several wrens
caught out of season
skim hoarfrost branches
without haste,
perilous flight, and all
the more luminous for it.

fireweed

    end of the day's heat
    undulates on a goldfinch,
    light drains
    into neon lime pin-pricks,
    fireflies launch
    from the the grassy tussock
    and wink over the island,
    sending on-again off-
    again signals of carnal purpose
    among soft-bodied beetles
    all gussied up
    for a night of summer sex
    in the yarrow and fireweed,
    lace and prim rose
    grace notes enfused with seduction,
    water on its way to steam.

high summer sun tracks small fish

in deep water
   minnows and their shadows
      visible but absent

     at the same moment

and with one movement
   reverse, dart & shiver
      through lilyreed anchors,

fleet and golden
   stream lined
      these small fish swimming

arc in noon dazzle
   as I circle this other side of presence
      called loss

how it will rise
   unbidden, slivers
      searching for a larger story.

three poems for a friend

for Sandra Purton

1. reprise

I suppose
we could look again at the summer
where things went wrong between us,
cedar, fir, dogwood greening-out
space the sky once held,
sound only a single bird call
and water falling
from great heights in slow time
on lichen and moss.

this continent between road and water
was rare,
smell of earth heavier
than the load we carried over
the path, descending through vines
and ferny torrent to the beach,
wet desert in fog
stretched between implacable cliffs.
hearing waves
through mist and showers,
persistent punishment
on figures moving to and fro,
you and I in lockstep
toward discord by then,
distracted by wet
wood, sick children,
listening but not hearing
what was really breaking up
on crusted rocks, there
at the edge of the sand.

The River
&
The Lake

        we left at high morning, walking
        down the shore to easier
        passage through forest vegetation
        no longer enchanting, merely vexing.
        weary with discomfort and unharmonious
        silence, we packed out gear soaked
        in salt water and resentment,
        taking away a little less
        than we had brought in,
        and went slowly east into the sun.

        for a time
        I tried to make it come out differently,
        tinkered with the chronology
        and rearranged the parts
        as one might want to change
        a painting of starfish in a rockpool —
        take a little off the bottom, say,
        so the balance suits better,
        repaint the surface
        in stronger light,
        trying to forget that failed paintings
        can never be fully recovered.

        now I know
        we are stuck,
        whether it's omission or fault
        that bound us in disagreement
        matters less than the
        small unalterable
        grit to be rubbed against
        from time to time,
        constant evidence of our attachment.
        lay it against dark inactivity
        yes, and all the miles between.

2. counterpoint

note against note
then mine alone, holding,
re-calibrated to wait
for awhile
but disinclined
to remain alone.
silence wholly audible
tells chaptered stories:
journey over cowled hills
in shoes worn from the outside of the heel in,
working the peel off an orange
in a spiral
as spring sun collects early bees
in reckless ventures,
altogether unaccountable.

now it's dusk
and you are listening to Ella Fitzgerald
singing back and forth
across a back-lit valley,
glassy air moving
nighthawks around the rim
on Ella's voice
in contrapuntal flight.

but you will deny all this,
say that you are caught again
in that thick woollen stillness
that takes you to the edge
of suffocation, and holds you there.
This is an old refrain
we both know by heart
and measure out in misapprehension.
I mean to reshape my part
into some sort of stubborness
I couldn't dignify by calling patience,
more like feigned indifference,
lighter, easier to lay aside.

The River
&
The Lake

3. ground-note

when it comes to signify
   a base of stone
      to lie beneath the swell and sway
      of early watermusic,

when regret becomes a burr
   I pull from my sock
      at the end of the day
         and drop in the woodstove

for its quick blaze,
   when the plan to make amends
      falls short for want of urgency
         or desire,

listen with care
   my dear old friend,
      for accord sufficient to the whole.
      low ascent. song.

shoring up

blue air thickens
shadowed by waiting,
cool nights
set as brilliants
   toward leaving

**The River
&
The Lake**

island

exchange of circular lapping,
wash the perimeter endlessly clean,
and cleaner,
justify it on either side
by stretched waves & over-
lay of firred horizon.
dwarf trees lean west for balance.

one path, textured
moss, navigates without instruments
among glint and fossils,
blue berry dots,
red starry lichen spills,
around and around the intricate empire
without reference to polar pull or disordered
future, one path
soft as parchment
threads its known way
and I, with a whole day rid of calamity
to track it.

promise

> *love's*
> *radical contour shines here in stillness*
> *secret, original, a dream of candor.*
>
> Phyllis Webb, "Two Pears: A Still Life"

    for the body
makes going beyond
the contentment of love
possible, your hand risen to my slick skin,
    reels of nerves tolling
  under its cut roundness

fever melts roses and ice into
    crisp night pools
 dark with mint, petalled.
our voices lie like spheres
    in some moon-raked orchard:
sites of circumnavigation.
fleshy windfalls, this time,
a bloom of juice,
    the taste of sun.

what finally happens

it takes so long
for the journey to reveal itself
distance only a point on a line
looking back

so long
to hear under white-city hum
the steady rhythm
drumming for this granite land

obdurate stubborn heart
half-cracked
but beating on
saying   stop
saying   listen
the seventh fire blazes
where you have been
on slag and clearcut
bloodied grouse
plastic and foil
and slicked seabirds on sand
a reproach of light
in oily darkness

takes so long
to understand that the land
has, finally, to teach us
its own dying
a gentle withdrawing
like a hand still curved
from another's touch
so little flesh
the bones shine through
with light enough
to take us forward
if we choose to go.

ACKNOWLEDGEMENTS

Versions of some poems appeared previously in *A Room of One's Own*, *Taproot*, *Quarry*, and *Alternatives Magazine*.

I owe thanks to family and friends, to the memory of my two mothers, Dorothy Bowles and Dorothy Page, whose love and support was unfailing. Thanks also to John Wadland for the best reading venue in the province, to Anne Corkett, Kathy Fretwell, Judith Mills, Sandra Purton, and Bronwen Wallace who helped shape the original manuscript. I'm grateful to Quarry Press, and especially to my editor, Carolyn Smart. Without her, this volume would lack title and its poems would be less true to the events they seek to recount.